BOILING IT DOWN:

THE ELECTRONIC POETRY CHAPBOOKS

OF LARRY D. THOMAS

BLUE HORSE PRESS   REDONDO BEACH, CALIFORNIA 2019

BOILING IT DOWN:

THE ELECTRONIC POETRY CHAPBOOKS

OF LARRY D. THOMAS

Blue Horse Press
318 Avenue I # 760
Redondo Beach,
California   90277

Copyright © 2019 by Larry D. Thomas
All rights reserved
Printed in the United States of America

Cover art: Jeffrey C. Alfier,
"Ruins, Terlingua, Texas"

Editors: Jeffrey and Tobi Alfier
Blue Horse Press logo: Amy Lynn Hayes (1996)

ISBN 978-0-578-42852-9

No part of this book may be reproduced or transmitted in any form or by any means, electronic or mechanical, including photocopy, recording, or any information storage and retrieval system now known or to be invented, without permission in writing from the publisher, except by a reviewer who wishes to quote brief passages in connection with a review written for inclusion in a magazine, newspaper or broadcast.

FIRST EDITION © 2019

This and other Blue Horse Press Titles may be found at www.bluehorsepress.com

This book is most appropriately dedicated to the author's friend and colleague, Dale Wisely, who, through his kindness and generosity, first published eleven of these fifteen collections of poetry.

Acknowledgments

Heartfelt thanks goes to Jeffrey and Tobi Alfier without whose kindness and generosity this book would not exist. Very special gratitude is extended to Jeffrey C. Alfier whose breathtaking photograph, "Ruins, Terlingua, Texas," graces the book's cover. Additional appreciation goes to the publishers/editors noted below who graciously permitted the author to reprint, in book form, the following electronic chapbooks:

With the Light of Apricots, Lily Press, Susan Culver (publisher/editor), 2007

Eros, *Slow Trains Literary Journal*/Samba Mountain Press, Susannah Indigo (editor), 2007

Plain Pine, *Right Hand Pointing*, Dale Wisely (publisher/editor), 2009

Five Lavender Minutes of an Afternoon, *Right Hand Pointing*, Dale Wisely (publisher/editor), 2010

Far (West Texas), *Right Hand Pointing*, Dale Wisely (publisher/editor), 2011

Social Networks, *Right Hand Pointing*, Dale Wisely (publisher/editor), 2012

Colors, *Right Hand Pointing*, Dale Wisely (publisher/editor), 2013

The Wadded Up Poem Behind the Dumpster, *Right Hand Pointing*, Dale Wisely (publisher/editor), 2014

Los Días de los Muertos, *Right Hand Pointing*, Dale Wisely (publisher/editor), 2015*

Jake & Violet, *Right Hand Pointing*, Dale Wisely (publisher/editor), 2016

El Padre, Virtual Artists Collective (nodding onion imprint), Steven Schroeder (publisher/editor), 2016

Plácido, Virtual Artists Collective (nodding onion imprint), Steven Schroeder (publisher/editor), 2016

Pecos, *Right Hand Pointing*, Dale Wisely (publisher/editor), 2017

"The Emperor of Ice-Cream" (after the poem by Wallace Stevens), *Right Hand Pointing*, Dale Wisely (publisher/editor), 2017

Luz (a demanding, elusive, and indomitable muse), *Right Hand Pointing*, Dale Wisely (publisher/editor), 2018

*"Irene," from *Los Días de los Muertos*, was nominated by *Right Hand Pointing* for the Pushcart Prize.

Contents

With the Light of Apricots   1-12

Eros   14-30

Plain Pine   32-51

Five Lavender Minutes of an Afternoon   55-73

Far (West Texas)   75-83

Social Networks   85-94

Colors   96-105

The Wadded Up Poem Behind the Dumpster   107-116

Los Días de los Muertos   118-130

Jake & Violet   135-151

El Padre   153-172

Plácido   175-189

Pecos   196-205

"The Emperor of Ice-Cream" (after the poem by Wallace Stevens)   208-217

Luz (a demanding, elusive, and indomitable muse)   219-229

About the Author   231

With the Light of Apricots

(for Dodie)

I. As if a God Had Ripped the Sundown

Remember

that morning
in the desert
when the sun
was a slice
of tangerine?
When we chewed
honeycombs,
our sunburned chins
dimpled and red
as cherries?
When, tipsy
on mimosas,
we wove
through the rosy
yellows of dawn
like mice
in a basket
of apricots?
When even
our teeth
were sweet?

Apricots

A few blocks off the plaza,
in the Santa Fe evening light
the color of brandy,
on the street below the branches
of the tree, they glowed in rosy,
yellow hues as if a god
had ripped the sundown, rolled it
into fuzzy, dimpled balls,
and flung them to the ground.
Fast as we could, deep
into the fabric of our shorts,
we crammed them till our pockets
sagged, and lumbered down
the darkening street
like lumpy angels, holy
with the light of apricots.

Five Houses Down

In a panic, the woman
at the day-care center
begged me to help her find them,
the two rowdy toddlers
who just moments before
squeezed through a rut beneath the fence
and toddled off. Their playmate
had seen them, and run to tell
the woman they had gone.
I found them five houses down,
standing beneath a tree of fruit,
some pieces of which were strewn
upon the ground. Each held his prized,
ripe apricot with both hands
as a man would a cantaloupe,
fumbling it in his palms
like a young god in training
sphering clay into a sun.

Fried Pies

To make the filling, the mothers
cut the ripened apricots from their stones,
slice them into strips, soak them in pots of water,
cook them, add sugar, cinnamon, and cook them
again till they reach just the right consistency.
As the filling cools, they roll out the dough
for the crust, cut it into round pieces
they spoon the filling into the middle of,
fold them neatly in half, seal the curved
edges, pressing them with the tines of a fork,
and deep-fry them in bubbling lard
to a perfect medium brown.
As the pies cool on the table,
the children close their eyes and salivate,
picturing a thousand ripe apricots
dangling from the branches of the trees,
each a fuzzy, rosy, yellow sun
setting in the maw of the night.

II. Their Skins of Rosy Yellow

Interlude Late in an Afternoon

For several days in a row, when I was home alone
in the waning hours of the afternoon, basking
in the shadows of the porch, she walked by
sans speaking, clad in a loose, cotton sundress
and barefoot. Her hair was straight, long and dark,
falling to her bare shoulders and back. One afternoon,
out of the blue, she stopped and queried whether
she could use my phone, only for a minute.
After her call, during which I never heard her speak,
she thanked me and left. The next afternoon,
a flush of embarrassment on her face and neck
ending at the shadow of her cleavage, she approached me
holding in her hand something wrapped in a paper towel.
Extending her offering and pressing firmly into my hand
whatever she had wrapped in the towel, she smiled. I felt,
oozing through the paper, the wetness of two apricots,
overripe, their skins of rosy yellow splitting, bleeding
onto my palm the sweet and sticky substance of a pass.

At the One of Solid Silk

Her unexpected death
two weeks ago
left him a widower
at twenty-five.
As night falls, as he has
at every dusk since she died,
he ghost-walks to her clothes
in the closet. He fingers
each of her blouses, lingering
at the one of solid silk,
a print of vivid, ripened apricots
lifelike as a detailed photograph
fit for framing, each apricot
crowned with drops of dew,
laden with her scent,
the blouse she wore
the moment his interest in her,
passing like a film fast-forwarded,
stopped, cropped to the frozen,
single frame of love.

The Picker

In the blur of a single motion,
she thrusts her hand into the branches,
clutches a cluster of ripened fruit,
snaps it from its stems, and lays it
bruiseless in the basket dangling
from her arm like a cheap straw purse.
She'll work like this till dusk, filling baskets
brimming with the promise of a better life.
At last, lumbering to her shanty
in the darkness, with bronze, aching hands
spared not even a moment for washing,
she'll ease her infant from the arms
of her grandmother, squeeze her to her breasts
for nursing, place her in a makeshift cradle,
cradle the weary head of her husband,
and collapse quickly asleep, her calloused
palm curled around the corner of her pillow,
redolent with the scent of apricots.

The Dream

For two years now, when he's slept in his cell at the state pen,
he's had the same, recurring dream. The apricots have ripened
on his front yard trees, bowing the branches so the lower ones
touch the ground. Frozen in his chair inside the window
like a quadriplegic, all he can do is watch as the crows descend
like a black, cawing cloud and devour the ripened fruit,
their beaks slashing like black knives. His trees bereft of fruit
and even leaves, he wakes, remembering how for miles around
the locals came to gaze upon the glory of his trees,
the largest and most productive in the county, bestowing
his dilapidated shanty with dignity, hiding it from the street
with a dense veil of fruit and leaves. He remembers how
he only meant to graze the big teenager who awoke him
late one night, stealing his apricots, but, firing an errant shot,
dropped him dead as a cold, pulpless apricot stone.

III. Fecund with the Promise

The Apricot Tree

Though it was established
with a grand root system
which drew its needed moisture
from deep within the earth,
he tended it daily
as a gardener would a rosebush.
He tracked the seasons with its foliage,
and took great pride in the imperceptible
widening of its trunk. Even in mid-
January, when its leafless branches
clacked in the howling wind
like the antlers of rutting stags,
he'd don his heaviest coat,
take his place on his porch,
and watch it through the afternoon
to dusk. Sans even moving, it creaked him
through the seasons like a wagon,
tugging him toward the summer
of his ninetieth year, toward dark green branches
bowed with the bounty of apricots, fecund
with the promise of baskets and damsels.

The Centenarians

Their gospel
 is the obvious.
They love
their weightless,
rawboned frames,
allowing them
ghostlike movement,
the inconspicuousness
of a mind
whooshing
through the rooms
of memory.
They cherish
their collections
of canes,
new and antique,
perfect for balance
or weaponry.
In the falseness
of their teeth,
they've found
their Truth,
reliable
as their diet
of rice, spring water,
and, canned,
dried, or fresh,
apricots.

Still Life

Of dried, cracked oil on canvas,
it hangs on a white wall, illumed
by the slanted beam of an early
afternoon spotlight-sun of track
lighting: a white table covered
with a white, cotton tablecloth;
a white porcelain plate; a knife
and fork of sterling silver;
and a fresh, ripe apricot
placed off-center on the plate.
Only the sheen of the plate
and its shadow distinguish it
from the tablecloth. The knife
and fork, lying equidistant
from the plate, draw the viewer's eye
to blade and tines, auguring
imminent violence. For the moment
intact, the peel of the apricot,
taut with the pressure of flesh,
pulses with the heat of pinkish yellow,
braced for the inevitable ravage
just beyond the canvas edge
of manicured, human hands.

Artificial Fruit

I saw them in a basket
on the table, in a slant
of late afternoon, winter
sunlight, a scrumptious cluster
of apricots so fresh their stems
were still attached, bearing, trembling
in a current of air from a vent,
browning leaves curling in the act
of dying. I stood there bothered
by their symmetry, too perfect
for actual fruit, so I bent
toward them, checking for redolence
or a bruise. Their plastic smell
gave them away, the telltale
sign of fraud. I felt a sadness
in their unbridgeable distance
from the real, imagining
their hollow desire, yea, longing
to trade their everlasting beauty
for even the transitory
dirge of decay, or clank of the knife
bounded against the stone of life.

Eros

I. Shackling the Body

Orgasm

The engine
of the id
at full throttle.
The apotheosis
of pulse

and breath.
For years
the body's
cells divide,
just, one day,

to reach it.
Reached,
it must be
reached
over and over

again,
shackling
the body
with ravishing
iron,

enslaving it
to a habit
the envy
of heroin.
And cocaine.

The Urge

It comes on
like the scratchy throat
and low grade fever
signaling a cold.

Soon, so intense
it's scary, it draws us
to the palpable darkness
of dank movie houses

we carve our way through
to grimy seats
as our shoes
make sucking sounds,

tugged from a concrete floor
sticky with spilled Coke
and God knows what else,
an *else* we don't even find

repulsive so desperate
is our need for relief
from the angel
plumed with love and violence.

Fingers

Clad in but your black,
silk kimono, you sit
on the sofa's edge as I
sit on the floor, facing you.
I slide your feet apart
a few inches, and,
with my right index finger,

trace the blue, pulsing veins
of your left foot.
As my finger
eases across your ankle
to your Achilles tendon
and starts its treacherous
journey up your calf

and around your knee
to your inner thigh,
you position on my scalp,
for imminent pressing,
your long, tapered nails
lacquered with the color
of crushed cherries.

Tongues

Today, while we're
apart, we won't
even notice them,
these autonomic,

vascular organs
enabling us
to taste, chew,
and speak.

Tonight,
warm with blood
and pulsing,
they will sneak

from their castles
of teeth,
caress
every atom

of our flushed,
forbidden flesh,
and swirl,
mellifluously

fluent
in the dark,
carnal language
of desire.

II. Redolent of Burgundy

Peach

Slightly overripe,
it dangles just above
my head. With the tips

of my thumb and fingers,
I clutch it,
pluck it from the tree,

and snap off its stem
with my teeth.
It bleeds a drop

of juice. The reds
and yellows of its skin
are softened

by its gossamer
of fuzz. Its fragrance,
still warm with sun,

makes my mouth water.
Just before I bite,
I see its cleft

beaded with dew,
flushed as your cleavage
after love.

Oyster

It lies on its shell, raw,
wet, and shiny. With a hint
of violence, I stab it

with a three-pronged fork,
slather it with cocktail sauce,
and lay it on a cracker.

As I ease it jiggling
to my tongue, it flares
my nostrils with the scent

of the sea. When I close
my eyes and bite, is it
the oyster I eat? Or you?

Fig

I lift it,
right before
your eyes,
from a bowl
of cool water.

Dripping wet,
so ripe
its bluish
purple skin's
begun to split,

its pink flesh
soft against
my thumbs
as your breast,
it fumes

its heavy
sweetness.
I tear it
apart, gaze,
and eat.

Never even
blinking,
you lick
its sticky juice
from my fingers.

By Candlelight

Their table is fragrant
with a spray of deep
red roses. As they wait
for the entrée, their hands
for the moment out of view,

they fondle the white linen
tablecloth. Droplets swell,
sponge the light, wobble,
slide down the stems, and pool
on the feet of their goblets.

They speak in hushed tones,
their breath musky,
redolent of burgundy.
Dinner is served.
As they slice, fork,

bite into a piece
of rare steak, and look up,
each sees the candle flame
flicker in the glazed,
expectant eyes of the other.

III. The Bull's-Eyed Heart

The Late Afternoon

I first took
notice of you
beneath your black
umbrella
was humid as drenched

gray terrycloth
wrung in the sky
by a giant,
phantom washerwoman,
spattering us

with fat, wobbling drops
of tepid rain.
It plastered your hair
to your forehead
like our sweat would

the first time
it mingled in darkness
and I looked down
at your closed eyelids,
your flared, pink nostrils,

your parted lips,
and your teeth streaked
with lipstick, quaking,
sunk into the blackness
of devourment.

Briefs

Carrying on
where we
left off,

they lie
crumpled
on the floor

beside the bed
in a shaft
of morning

sunlight,
yours on top
of mine,

their crotch
fibers
saturate

with the smell
of us,
candied here

and there
with our
secretions.

The Bed

We somnambulate
the tedium of hours
clotting the day
just to make it

to the darkness
where it waits,
unmade, fuming
our scent, archiving

the blasts of our furnace-
breath, keeping the shape
of palms, heels,
knees, and buttocks,

coaxing our skin,
even in our absence,
again and again,
to fire.

Eros

He's just a young, winged
boy whose bow and arrows
are ever at the ready.

His arrows are golden,
animate with the feathers
of doves, or leaden,

listless with the feathers
of owls. Singling out
his next, unsuspecting

victim, whether god or mortal,
he pulls an arrow
at random from his quiver,

fixes its notch flush
against horsehair, stretches
the bowstring till it frays,

and shoots, invading
the bull's-eyed heart
with doom or craving.

Plain Pine

Bloodsong

At but the faintest hint
of daybreak
Pauline wakes before Amos
and lies mummy-still
beneath the quilts
of old women.
She wakes to nothing
but a world
outside her shack
of a gradual
hemorrhaging of dawn,
dew-chilled,
and the high roostings
of songbirds
loosening their grip
on scabbed branches
and hurtling
the plumed missiles of bodies
electric with blood
to nothing
but morning sky.

Her Black Iron Skillet

Pauline lays
a floured slab
of venison
in the crackling grease
of her black
iron skillet,
tilts her head
slightly back,
clasps floured hands
caking them together
with the blood
of wild game,
and readies her nostrils
for the deep,
steamy draughts
wafting the very soul
of wood
and fresh meadow.

Watercolors

With warm roses
dawn blushes
plump cheeks
moist with the steam
of hot coffee
and dances
in a beard.
Eyes water
from the brilliance
of early light
as bristled ears
resonate with wet
birdsong.
Awash with dew
scuffed boots creak
trampling toward a coop
where a pastel hand
will tear the head
from a damp,
clucking pullet.

Nothing but Music

As he licks
his last rib
Amos belches
and his bristled
nostrils flare.
He opens a biscuit
like a fat book
and mops
the last thick puddle
of pork grease
from his platter.
Amos belches again
and he grins
thinking of the morning
he and his brother
killed the big red hog
whose squeals
ringing through the woods
were nothing but music
to their bristled
human ears.

Cool Water

The bedclothes
damp with the sweat
of human sickness,
Pauline wrenches her body
in troubled dream-sleep.
Even the moonglow
is nothing but frost
where the pines
with their bark
of glazed ice
keep creaking
in the night.
Amos hears them
through the shack walls
and he hears
the labored breathing
of his wife
delirious
with high fever.
She wakes refusing
his raspy offer
of a sip
of cool water,
licks the slight bleeding
of heat-split lips,
and braces her delirium
for his mount.

The Dark Child

Their shack hunkers
deep, deep in the woods
and its tin roof creaks
with the coming cold.
Her long, loosened braids
are oiled with the bronze
of her body ooze.
She jerks in her nightmare
with her back next to his,
his overalls crumpled
in the chair beside him,
stinking, stiffening
with the blood of wild doves.
Their fire dies as they sink
deeper and deeper into sleep,
the black night scooting in close
like a dark, whimpering child.

Plain Pine

As Pauline sleeps
in the dawn-glow
Amos studies
her unfinished pair
of miniature buzzards.
He can't help
but notice
how their perfect heads
stretch skyward
on thin, naked necks
and their half-
whittled wings
struggle violently
in the knots
of plain pine
like the straining
arms of men
freeing themselves
from a pit
of quicksand,
these tiny
wooden buzzards
already putrid
with the dark
gift of life
his very wife
is giving them.

The Stare

Amos is half-drunk
deep in the woods
in the violet haze
of twilight.
A crow thrashes,
her broken wing
stuck in underbrush.
Amos nears her
with caution.
The black fires
of her eyes
so like his wife's
are still raging,
unforgiving,
still straining muscles
in her skull,
finally fixing themselves
in the unrelenting gaze
of her black,
exquisite stare.

Where Brothers Walk

clouds are stacked
in a sky
like slabs
of wild meat,
and a sun
wobbles up,
squints whiskey-
bloodshot eyes,
glints the stubble
of double chins,
and warms
the guiltless grins
of Red, Amos,
and the dark
crooked limb
bridging thick
right shoulders
where a gutted
buck sways.

Red

As she shaves
the last pine talon
with her sharp blade
she sees the bloody
white apron of Red,
her husband's brother.
Even the evening sky
under which she sits
on an old stump
is spattered blood-red
by the dying sun.
In the deep red light
she shaves it half-sunk
in the detailed eye
of a cottontail.
She shaves it
with the strength,
in the red brick
slaughterhouse,
of Red's sledgehammer
cracking the skulls
of fat cattle.

Hummingbirds

With fresh pine
Red and Amos
are framing out
Red's little houses
for his pit bulls.
Red loves
sinking big nails
deep into the soft
yellow pine
with but three
or four blows
of his hammer,
but Amos
keeps hitting the knots,
bruising his left thumb
till it bleeds,
ruining big nails
on the little hearts
of Pauline's hushed,
uncarved hummingbirds.

In the Next Room

Pauline wakes
in a sweat
and stares
at a wall
in the next room
where a moon
casts sharp
black shadows
of her carvings' beaks
and flawless claws.
She wakes
to nipples
grown taut
with moonglow
and the memory
of animal touch.
Though she shoved him
violently away
her animal breasts
still shudder
with the warmth,
the savage warmth
of Red's cupped,
adulterous hands.

The Pyracantha

where early morning sounds
are muffled
in the damp gray fleece
of a fog
where Pauline searches
for just the right
chunk of pine
for her redbird,
where suddenly
she sees clusters
of bright orange berries
where Red tossed
the torn shreds
of his daughter's clothes
and the child
in mute terror
fixed wide eyes
on the bright berries,
on bright clusters
of the mute
stunned beaks
of lady redbirds.

Blackie

As she pries
the last bloody pup
from the bleeding womb
of her pit bull bitch,
she catches
the distant yelling
of her father
and his fighter friends.
She sees the light
of their lanterns
dancing in their wide
excited eyes
as they crowd
the pit's edge
and shine their light
on the scarred terror
of Blackie,
the pups' father,
as Red
pries Blackie's jaws
from his dangling
opponent's
scarlet,
wet velvet throat.

Contours

Red's daughter
sleeps with the pine,
fist-sized owl
Pauline gave her for Christmas.
She dreams of it
nuzzling the warmth
between her breasts
in a windowpaned square
of warm moonglow.
With her breast flesh
she feels the contours
of a beak
curved for murder,
so magnificent,
so sure,
chilly as the machinery
of her father's love.

Dream-Trap

Red struggles
in his sleep
like a leashed
pit bull.
He sniffs
the faint stain
of first light
as his bristled
ears twitch
for the blood-
curdling crowing
of his gamecocks.
His bugged,
bloodshot eyes jerk
loosening thick
red lashes
glued with sleep,
rip lids apart
like fresh cuts
and slurp the crack
of dawn.

The Hiding Place

As if asleep
Pauline waits
in her bed
for Red's
drunk pounding
on her latched
screen door,
for the drunk
pounding
and her niece
crouching
in her studio
in the moon-
flung shadows
of shuddering crows.

Pinfeathers

In the pitch-dark,
in the wee hours
of her niece's birthday
Pauline dreams
of the birthdays
coming to her niece
with each quartet
of the seasons,
coming to her niece
like little blue spots
in the warm flesh
of young bird wings,
little blue spots
sprouting from flesh
with the promise
of large blue feathers,
the brilliant blue comings
of the birthdays
which not even Red
can stop.

The Big Red Rooster

was a gift to Amos
from his brother.
Pauline was home alone
late that night
and she still sees
her bedroom light
raging in an eye
pupilled with the bead
of her rifle.
She still sees
the big red rooster
thrashing on its back
and its grand wings
staked to the earth
with black paws,
and she still feels
her right index finger
freezing at the trigger
and herself
just standing there
and watching
as the one-eyed skunk
closed in for the kill.

Her Untowelled Woods

are still drenched
from a shower
of wild rain.
Pauline walks barefoot
to the spot
where lightning
just hours before
struck her tallest pine
and burned it
to the black earth.
She squats
near the stump
whose fat
scabby roots
are the feet
of a huge crow
the last of its kind
still hunkering
ever closer
to the black earth,
still smoldering,
still mustering up
its final
bloodcurdling caw.

Five Lavender Minutes of an Afternoon

Preface

Of my 16 published collections of poetry, *Five Lavender Minutes of an Afternoon* is the first dedicated to my early childhood. In my poetry, I have turned to the natural world for my subject matter much more than I have turned to the human, especially the actual or even imaginary lives of my closest relatives. The reasons for this are many, not the least of which is my reluctance to invade the privacy of those who over the years have meant so much to me and who, in so many ways, made me what I am. Not until each person in these twelve poems was long deceased was I able to write about them.

When I think of a single word which best characterizes the lives of my parents and grandparents, it is without question "hard." Three of my grandparents came from Tennessee to West Texas in the late 1800s (my paternal grandfather was born in Texas), and they came in covered wagons. The lives they eked out as tenant farmers in that desolate and harsh environment were unbelievably humble and difficult, yet three of my grandparents survived into their mid-eighties and the fourth to the age of seventy-nine. Their strong character and hard physical lives sustained them. Both of my parents had to drop out of school in the ninth grade to work the cotton fields, and remained tenant farmers until their early thirties when my father went to work at and ultimately owned a service station. My father was forty and my mother thirty-nine when I was born.

My father worked ten to twelve-hour days, seven days a week at his service station. This left the child-rearing to my mother who raised four sons, the eldest of whom was twenty years older than the youngest. Consequently, she had a child enrolled in public school for thirty-one consecutive years. In addition to raising her children, she also hand-washed, starched and ironed the service station uniforms for my father and kept our modest house anal-retentively clean.

I chose "Five Lavender Minutes of an Afternoon" as the title poem of this collection because I felt it captured my mother's selfless dedication to everyone in her family. For five fleeting minutes that afternoon, she steeped her difficult life in the sensual pleasures so long denied her, and, as I and my little brother, Bobo, did with our balsa wood planes, she "flew."

Red-Letter Epiphany

Its cover was worn,
white leather, scuffed
as the bull hide boots
of a working cowhand.

I'll never forget
the first time I held it,
looked to see if Mama
were around, and opened it.

What few books Mama had
were prized, off-limits to me
and Bobo, my kid brother,
till we made it to first grade

and learned to read.
I'd never seen onionskin,
and loved the way it felt
between my thumb and fingers.

When Mama yelled, I jerked,
gripped the forbidden book
for a split second
by a single page

of onionskin, and heard it
tear from the spine
as the rest of the New
Testament crashed to the floor.

I stood frozen, holding
a fragment of onionskin
with words red as cardinals
trembling in a field of snow.

Hell Yes I Believed

After the wiener roast, Mama shoved me
so close to the church retreat campfire
my eyeballs burned like the skin of a bather
fallen asleep for hours in midday sun.
She grabbed my little hand, thrust it
dangerously near the smoldering mesquite,

and whispered, "Look and don't blink!"
Said hell would be a thousand times hotter
and, worse than that, everlasting.
For weeks I awoke in a sweat,
shriveling, blackening and twisting
like a marshmallow bubbling on a stick.

Though she meant well, she'd just as soon
have branded my brain with the red-
orange iron of disbelief, the way,
for the next few years of my life,
just to function, I denunciated
heaven to quench the flames of hell.

"Mama Sug"
(in memory of Margaret Ann Elizabeth Cisco Coleman)

Of blocks of native Texas limestone,
the house they kept on their slim pension
was built in the 1800's.
Summer afternoons, unpretentious
as the dough each morning at first light

she'd pummel with her fists into biscuits,
she'd waddle her weary corpulence
to the rocker on her wooden porch,
her slat bonnet tied in a bow
snug against the flab of her throat.

For her own burial, so as not
to burden her children or grandchildren,
she kept what little cash she'd saved
rolled in a cotton pouch and safety-
pinned to what was left of her bra.

Although ever clad in a long cotton dress
and brown cotton hose she rolled down
the tops of just below her knees,
she never wore corsets or underdrawers,
prudently comforting her womanhood

ravaged by conjugal obligations
and the savage natural births
of ten children. Even the snuff
she'd pack into her labial vestibule
with a flat wooden spoon, was Honest.

Grandma's House

Like the remnants of a frontier fort,
only its thick limestone walls still stand.
Its little town of Seymour was
severe, setting in a single year
the Texas records for heat and cold.

Winters, its gas space heater glowed
like a candlelit jack-o'-lantern.
During blue northers, we'd back
up against it till our trousers smoked
and the hairs on our calves crinkled.

The old house was drafty, the back
bedroom so cold the toilet bowl
water froze, and when we gasped "geez,"
it whistled from our lips in frost.
We'd slide between the icy sheets

beneath the quilts and shiver
till our bodies made a warm spot.
Grandma heated bricks in her oven
and wrapped them in burlap for our feet
trembling in the dark like trapped rabbits.

To Rid Our Bodies of Red Dust

The first time Bobo and I
laid eyes on a body of water
it scared us, so scarce it was
in far West Texas where we grew up.

We resided in Midland,
midway between Fort Worth and El Paso,
a hundred long miles from the nearest
running river or manmade lake.

For an outing, to rid our bodies
of red dust, Mama and Dad would take us
to San Angelo, to the Concho River.
Before Dad hit the brakes of the old Buick,

we'd freed ourselves of shoes, socks,
Levi's, shirts, and modesty, ready to jump
off the riverbank. The soft mud
was a blessing, oozing between our toes

like poop in a chicken coop.
Clad with but our oldest pairs
of threadbare Fruit-of-the-Looms,
we'd dunk one another repeatedly

in the brownish-green water, splashing
and diving to exhaustion,
the Concho so much better
than the frightening waters of baptism.

Five Lavender Minutes of an Afternoon

Mother Worrell, Dad's paternal grandmother,
was the sledge which drove the spike of religion
deep into the huge, virgin heart of Mama.

From then on, for the better part of five decades,
Mama felt she never measured up to the Beatitudes.
Despite her fervor in attending church services

at least three times per week and her diligence
in keeping the house alien to cigarettes or a single
can of beer, she wallowed in the mire of shame,

save five minutes of the afternoon following
another day of grammar school when Bobo and I
walked into the den and found her reclining

sideways on the sofa, her head propped up by her arm.
Her hair freshly coiffed, her body clad in a stylish
lavender evening gown ending at her heels,

she greeted us with forced sophistication, inquiring
how our day had gone. As she spoke, she took, deep
into her lungs, drags off a long, filtered Lucky Strike,

exhaling smoke rings wobbling like haloes
above her fine coiffure before unraveling in the air.
Too shocked to speak, we watched her act as if nothing

were unusual, taking deep drags, exhaling.
After a few minutes, she sat up on the sofa, crunched
the cigarette into a brand-new lavender ashtray,

laughed, and said she was just kidding. As she laughed,
the last of her smoke rings hovered for a moment
above her head and vanished, fleeting as her stint in sin.

Dad-Eyes

Dad always took great pride in how, of his four sons,
I was the one who, in looks, most resembled him.
He wore a wide, thick cowboy belt of cowhide
hand-tooled with oak leaves and acorns. Each morning,

seven days a week, after he pulled on, zipped, and buttoned
the trousers of his service station uniform, he'd thread
the belt through the loops and cinch it tight with the buckle.
I never noticed it until the first of those nights he came home

late from work and woke me and Bobo from our fitful sleep.
Those were the nights he drank the liquor he kept hidden
in the glove compartment of his work car. It took the dad-eyes
Bobo and I were used to, and turned them into something

strange and wild, much like the shiny, plastic ones of the stuffed
lion his big game hunter friend kept in his den to show off
to his guests. Those were the nights he unbuckled the belt,
pulled it from his trousers, folded it in half, and whipped us.

Bobo just stood stoically in place, holding back his big,
wobbling tears, but I ran to the bathroom and coiled myself
like a snake around the base of the toilet, not because
I was afraid but to provide something between me

and the cowhide to take the blows and keep me from hating him.
Over time, I still learned to love him and knew he loved me.
To this day, in the cobalt heavens of my memories,
those blows still shine the brightest and most distant of the stars.

Balsa Wood

With two wings, a fuselage,
and a tail, all of balsa wood,
we'd construct our little planes,
the wings and tails so thin
we'd scissor their plastic sheaths
painstakingly as Mama
cutting coupons from the Sunday paper.

Through a slot in the side
of the fuselage, we'd slide the main wing,
toward the front for gliding,
the back for loops. The tail
slid into a groove atop the back.
Sometimes, the fierce West Texas wind
would dislodge the tail, causing the plane

to cartwheel over rocks and cacti
till the wings broke like dry kindling.
We'd patch them if we could with Scotch tape
and throw their weightless mass to the wind,
clenching our fists as if our lives
hinged on the next safe landing.
And at the age of ten, they did.

Baby Horny Frogs
(Texas Horned Lizards)

We'd stand them on dimes,
turn them on their backs,
and coax them asleep
stroking their bellies
gently with the tips

of our forefingers.
Kay's finger was long
and slender, its nail
bright with red polish.
I'll never forget

the day she asked me
to lie on my back
on red sand beneath
the stand of mesquites
just outside the view

of my vigilant
mother, watching us
intermittently
through the small window
above her kitchen

sink. I swear it burned,
that edge of Kay's nail,
circling my navel,
stirring my blood toward
anything but sleep.

Of Loaves and Fishes

A couple of weekends a year,
when Dad could get away
from his Mobil service station,
he, I, Bobo, and Mama
would leave the Midland flatland
graced by neither hill nor tree,
and head to Balmorhea Lake.
The lake's farthest silver edge

lapped the lavender majesty
of the Davis Mountains.
We stayed on its steep, rocky shore
in an aluminum travel trailer.
Mama baked our bread to save expense.
One fretful Sunday afternoon,
the day after I reached puberty
and learned that Dad knew it,

he, Bobo, and I were fishing for bass
in the middle of the lake.
We hadn't caught a single fish
since the night of our arrival.
From the squinted corner of my eye,
I watched Dad's lips for the faintest
hint of movement, my only warning
of the fateful words of a father

to a son hooked in the leaden depths
of manhood, when, all of a sudden,
our three rods bowed with bass, the start
of a catch so grand it took our stringer
and the bottom of the boat to hold it,
enough fish to feed, the rest
of my adolescence, the throngs
of bleak silence between us.

Lake Balmorhea
(far West Texas)

As we rowed out
to the middle of the lake to fish,
we'd watch Mama growing smaller,
sitting on a rock at the lake's edge.

She'd sit for hours,
staring at the distant Davis Mountains,
her gaze intent as a playwright's
fixed on the first performance

of her masterpiece,
a complex play which,
because she penned it,
only she understood,

each mountain a character
miraculous in the blue
of development, ravishing
in the changing, desert light.

The Wallet

Dad's life, though not once did I ever
hear him say it, was hard. His hands
were its testaments: thick as dark
Bibles with cracked, buffed covers,
blotched with dried blood. He never
wore gloves. Said they tore too easily
and were a waste of money, of bills

so scarce he'd carry for years the same
wallet, opening it only to change out
his driver's license and State Farm card.
Once I gave him one for Christmas.
Two years later, he gave it,
still in its box, to my oldest brother
for his birthday; my oldest brother,

who, two years after that, wrapped it
and gave it back to me for Christmas.
When I noticed it looked familiar,
we laughed so hard, all three of us,
we cried, the hands I wiped my eyes with
embarrassingly smooth, useless,
untried as the calfskin in the box.

Far (West Texas)

1

the miles
between the eyes
of a horse

2

the long
dirt road
between Lust
and Love

3

the church
is Catholic:
the desert
drifts down
to the pews
like the laying
on of hands

4

visitors
are occasional,
unexpected,
each a major city

5

the only
thing to do
is be

6

noise
is the beetle
gnawing at
the brain:
silence,
the miraculous
journey
to the bleached,
immaculate skull

7

the cistern
howls
like breath
blown over
a bottle,
dredging up
its memory
of rain

8

the hawk
shrieks:
the cloudless sky
recoils,
scrambling
in our eyes

9

parsimony
is mayor,
judge,
and governor:
politics,
the paring down
by sun
and wind
to dust

Social Networks

1

cyberspace:
friends
spreading gossip
sans the warmth
of bad breath

2

before a sold-out,
wide-eyed audience,
knockout punches
landing with the sound
of falling snow

3

libel
whooshing at the speed
of light

4

gawking
at the art
of conversation
in its death throes

5

five hundred friends
simultaneously
feigning fascination
with what I ate
for breakfast

6

messaging
sans the drag
of reflection
or the arduous
application
of syntax

7

words
languishing in the shadows
cast by tone of voice
and body language

8

profiles
ballooning and reveling
on a dance floor
where the actual
is anathema

9

ID thieves
believing again
in Santa Claus

10

fiction
deconstructing
in the luminous
absence
of good & evil

Colors

Red

Crayon
of violence.
Of the spectrum,
long wave extreme.

Candy-
apple-radiance
of flowing,
arterial blood.

In the zoo
of light,
the lion
pacing in the ruby's cage.

Unction of war.
Passion
in a seizure
of dazzle.

Yellow

Soul
of daffodil
and ripe
lemon.

Hue
of cheer.
Makes blue
green with envy.

Meditating
with red
into the zen
of orange.

Belly laugh
of cowardice
yet jackets
the wasp.

Blue

Aloof denizen
of sky
and sea
of the wave-

length four seven five
millimicrons
shouldered
by violet

and green. Psycho-
logically
primary.
Pluralized, the jokes

of God
anguishing
between staves
of music.

Frozen fire
of sapphire.
Cool
as hell.

Purple

Consolatory
Heart
of the wounded

warrior.
Lush appellation
of the profane

firing the quartz,
lidless eyes
of demons

gleaming in a hell
of amethyst.
Blue

injuring red
with deep
bruises,

richening
into crimson
and scarlet

to sop
the murderous cloth
of royalty.

Green

Liquor of freshness.
Water-
color wash

of spring.
Spry child
of Blue

and mischievous
Yellow. The hushed
giggle of cousins

cavorting
in the emerald's
treehouse.

The shade
of their sweet,
astonishing guilt.

Orange

Red spellbound
with an afterthought
of yellow.

Habitant
of flame.
Fetid

breath-glow
of snaggletoothed
jack-o'-lantern.

Popsicle bliss.
Wedges
of planets

of fruit
teeth-blasted
into bitter-

sweet explosions
of succulent
novas.

Black

Nomenclature
of the plague.
Bestows the dog

with melancholy,
the cat
with bad luck.

Achro-
matic amalgam
of red, yellow

and blue.
Blush
of death.

White

Blinding absence
of light.
Gray

so very light
it's hardly gray
at all.

Color
of zero
saturation.

Pallor
of milk
and snow.

Of Hue, Shade, Tint and Value

The bright
shiny red
of the skin
of the apple
I am sinking

my gleaming
teeth into
isn't really
red at all
but just

the light
the skin
reflects
beyond
what's only

seemingly
so brightly,
shiningly
and intrinsically
red.

Day-Glo

The apogee
of ecstasy.
On the young girl

with a nose ring,
the poetry
of chartreuse hair

topping out
a body
of shapeless prose.

The Wadded Up Poem Behind the Dumpster

1.

It is cocooned
in its own
shadows.

2.

Wet, it meditates
on the rain
for several hours
before returning
to its restful
desiccation.

3.

Its letters
languor in the paper
house of mirrors.

4.

A stray dog
sniffs it
for a momentary
epiphany;
it prays
he doesn't pee.

5.

Late at night
a bobcat
swats it
with his paw
as if it were
a ball of yarn.

6.

Its verbs
grow restless
in their creased
straitjackets,
annoying
its nouns.

7.

A street person
ponders
picking it up,
but leaves it alone,
fearing it might
complicate matters.

8.

Bleaching out
and growing brittle
from the sun,
its words
begin their pilgrimage
to the shrine
of dust.

9.

Its imperceptible turning
to pale yellow
is the greatest
of its countless joys.

10.

Just before its words
bleed and fade
beyond recognition,
a toddler
uncrumples it,
relishing
each letter
as if it were
her favorite toy.

Los Días de los Muertos

(Big Bend National Park area, far West Texas)

I. All Hallows' Eve
(October 31st)

The Dugout

Three-fourths of it
loom below ground level.
It began as a mine shaft
but was quickly deserted
for another site. The portion
above ground is adobe brick,
a six-foot high mesquite door,
and horizontal windows
on three of the four walls.
The roof is corrugated iron;
the floor, uneven Mexican tile.
Irene says she and Helga wallow
in the belly of Mother Desert,
regarding their humble abode
as a "dress rehearsal" for Death:
a living grave bathed here
and there with the light
of sun, moon, and star.

Felines

Outside the dugout,
the branches
of an old mesquite
creak with an unkindness
of ravens, preening.
The early sun,
with its luminous,
unkempt fingernails,
is prying through
a film of dust
on wavy windowpanes.
Helga contemplates
whether to wake
her ill mother, Irene,
or let her sleep.
Seven stray cats
languish at the foot
of her chair
like an oval rug
fashioned of the black
pelts of rabbits.

Irene

ponders the abuse
she suffered as a child.
The nights were long,
bereft of a single star.
Mother Desert, far away,
awaited her arrival,
much more magical
than fairy tales of wolves,
witches, deceit, murder:
a place where darkness
sparkled with the light
of five thousand stars
and animals, with nothing
but will, breath, and clay,
pulsed their soft survival.

Helga

was an accomplished artist
before the tremors came,
rendering her right hand useless
for the steadiness and control
of crayon, pen, or brush.
The tremors had slithered
down the bloodline of her father,
silent vipers saturating
the flesh of her soul with venom.
Irene took her in, nurturing
the remnants of her genius
with good books and the pleasure
of conversation ever fresh,
provocative, and engaging.
Each grew to love the other's
companionship so much that
neither felt the dubious need
for pastor, close friend, or lover.

II. All Saints' Day
(November 1st)

Curandera

Her face
is a shadow
framed by a scarf
of black lace.
Her dress,
also of black lace,
is ankle-length,
and rustles
as she moves
about the dugout.
She slowly
circles Irene
who sits entranced
in her rocker
of mesquite.
Undulant as a dancer,
the *curandera* moves,
leaving in her wake
the scent of lemon grass,
garlic, and wellness.

With Her Hands

in an antique
Mexican bowl,
Helga kneads
the white paste
of sugar, water,
and meringue powder.
Feigning sleep,
Irene listens for,
like fresh snow
squeezed into
a snowball,
the crunching sound
the paste will make
as Helga,
after kneading it
to just the right
consistency,
presses it
into the mold
of a plastic
human skull.

Marigolds

Each spring, Helga
plants their seeds
in terra cotta pots so,
when the nights turn cold,
she can move them
inside the dugout.
As she carries them
to their place in the sun,
they tremble
so thick with orange
and yellow blooms
she can't see their stems.
In hours, like torches
of orange and yellow flame,
they will light the way
for the spirits of the dead
to their gravesites,
redolent with fresh food
and the warm embraces
of those they left behind.

Clemente

As she adorns the sugar skulls
with pink, green, and purple icing,
Irene selects the most promising
for his name. She will write it
in flowing, purple cursive,
remembering how he tutored her
in all things Mexican; the Aztecs,
Mayans, Toltecs, the Blue House
of Frida and Diego, the pyramids,
and the flaming murals of *Los
tres grandes*: Orozco, Siqueiros
and Rivera. The love of her life,
he visits her often in thought and spirit.
She still hears the creaking wheels
of the mule-drawn wagon
bearing his casket: the alternate
laughing and sobbing of his friends
and loved ones half-drunk on tequila,
ambling behind the wagon to his grave
to celebrate his life as they took turns
shoveling Mother Desert over his casket,
returning him to the only Mother
he ever knew. When dawn breaks,
Irene will walk to his gravesite
and ready it for his imminent visit.

III. All Souls' Day
(November 2nd)

The Altar

Of tiered concrete painted white,
near the entrance to the cemetery,
it was erected by the locals
solely for the celebration
of *Los Días de los Muertos*.
This evening, as night falls
like the laying on of hands,
it will be radiant with the light
of a bonfire casting long shadows
across the graves, the shadows
of the expectant living waiting
for the presence of the dead.
This morning, Irene is kneeling
at the altar, easing mementos
of Clemente from her colorful bag
woven by a Mexican artisan.
She gently sets them on the shrine:
black, antique prayer beads;
a tuft of his blue-black hair
sealed in a heart of acrylic;
his heirloom jar of puppies' teeth;
his favorite book of poems;
a pot of dazzling marigolds;

the sugar skull made even sweeter
by the purple icing of his name;
a long stemmed, blood-red rose;
and a photo of him and Irene
dancing in a moment frozen
in time and kept for the ages
in a gilded frame of Mexican silver.

Clemente's Gravesite

is as plain
as his unpretentiousness.
Weeks before he died,
he asked that it be covered
with a cairn of local rocks
and marked with nothing
but a cross of mesquite
with only his first name
carved across the transverse.
He felt Mother Desert
was sufficient to serve
as a monument.

The Procession

Led by a mule-drawn wagon
carrying the elderly,
it moves toward the cemetery
like a dark, turgid river
glinting here and there
with tinsel and little candles.
Irene and Helga walk behind
the wagon, clad in black dresses,
smiling beneath their masks of skulls.
The children are laughing,
rattling toy caskets and skeletons,
their cheeks smeared with the icing
of sugar skulls. In joyous
solemnity, the living walk,
erasing with each, sure step
the specious border between life
and death. Laden with food,
incense, mementoes, blood-red roses,
and flickering candles, they walk,
followed by children clutching
pots of marigolds glowing
in the incipient darkness
like armloads of harmless fire.

The Visitation

The chilled cemetery air
is fragrant with *mole negro*,
tamales, *pan de los muertos*,
and burning incense. Darkness
is falling on paths aglow
with marigolds and candles.
Glasses of *pulque* and tequila
clink in deferent toasts.
It is 6 p.m., and the bells
begin to ring to summon
the sacred spirits. A bonfire
lifts burning cinders to the sky.
At Clemente's grave, the cross
and kneeling countenances
of Irene and Helga cast
trembling shadows. In time,
Clemente's spirit will join them,
so palpable it could easily
be mistaken for the wind.

Jake & Violet

(Terlingua, far West Texas)

Preface

My best friend of my early adulthood served as a medic in the Vietnam War. Although he never carried weapons, he saw their carnage all about him: in the motionless, silent violence of amputated arms and legs; in heavy bandages scarlet with fresh blood; and in the wild eyes of the lucky yet maimed survivors, eyes which would never again know the peace of normalcy.

Although I know he trusted me as much as he had ever trusted anyone, he never said a word about his war experiences. When I told him he could talk and I would listen, if he ever needed to get anything off his chest, he would simply look at me and break into an almost imperceptible smile. He never even spoke about the "jungle rot" which gnarled his toenails, visible only when he wore his beloved Mexican *huaraches*. He was one of the gentlest, most caring souls I ever knew.

Only once, when I and his wife (who was also my friend) were alone, she queried whether she could tell me something in strictest confidence. I replied, "Absolutely." She then told me about the countless nights her husband had awaken screaming at the top of his lungs; about his night sweats so profuse they saturated and stained their bedclothes. Only out of concern for her personal welfare, I asked if he had ever been physically violent toward her, and she said she would never talk about that even if it happened because she loved him more than life itself.

Note to the reader: The characters and events in this collection of poems are solely derived from the author's creative imagination. Any ostensible reference to an actual person or event in these poems is completely unintended.

Dedication

To the brave who die a thousand deaths…

1. The Tenuous Borders

With the Seldom Help

Jake, with the seldom help
of a neighbor or two,
built their one-room adobe
over the course of two years.
He suffers from PTSD
and lives off SSI benefits.
His wife, Violet, receives

a slim Social Security pension
from forty years of work
as a nurse's aide in Del Rio.
After his military service,
Jake, although a jack-of-all-
trades, never held a steady job
but clandestinely, so as not

to lose his SSI benefits,
did odd jobs as his mental state
allowed. Violet grew up
near Terlingua; Jake, at the edge
of Del Rio where he lived
all his life before settling
with Violet in Terlingua.
For two years now,

they've started their day
with coffee at their small,
Mexican table in the adobe.
As they sip, Mexico looms
just to the south of them
like a mute, staring stranger.

Valium

To prevent his savage
episodes, Jake's doctor
prescribed a maximum
dose of Valium.

It stilled his lips
and slowed the blinking
of his eyes,
keeping his face

blank as his bedsheets.
He barely even breathed.
As the dosage was reduced
over the grueling course

of several days, Violet
watched his brutal crawl
toward the distant homeland
of his Self, a Self infected

with the ineradicable,
though sometimes
prayerfully dormant,
virus of violence.

Outpatient

The pen the doctor used
to sign Jake's hospital release

was heavy as a judge's pen
freeing a man from prison

though not from the shackles
of parole. As Violet wheeled him

to the hospital van, the morning
sunlight seemed unusually bright,

their weary eyes wincing
like an infant's in a stroller.

Unbeknownst to the other,
each mused the hollow meaning

of "out," the "out" forever welded
to the implacable steel of "patient."

Phantoms

It is mid-July, three
o'clock in the afternoon.
In the hot shade
of her adobe porch,
Violet is gazing

out over the desert.
The heat waves shimmer
from the desert floor
like phantom serpents,
blurring the edges

of creosote, ocotillo,
prickly pear and mesquite.
Even her breathing
is labored as she languishes,
baking like a biscuit

in a low-heat oven.
She reminisces the time
she met Jake in his Del Rio
hospital room.
Heavily medicated,

he hardly noticed her
moving about the room
like a phantom,
blurring the tenuous
borders between them.

2. Steeped in the Ages Old Secrets of the Desert

PTSD
(post-traumatic stress disorder)

Sometimes, Jake goes all day
without speaking. He walks
back and forth along the south
wall of the adobe, stopping
now and then to stare

out the window as if the stranger
were approaching from Mexico.
These are the times Violet
dares not mention a memory,
keeping quiet as possible,

knowing even a glance at Jake
can detonate an imaginary
IED. She waits patiently
for the Jake she loves to return,
the Jake with feelings, not

this Jake cold as a side of beef
suspended on a meat hook,
waiting for the cleaver,
the chopping into chunks
tossed to the lions of his dreams.

The Shadow

Jake is somewhere
outside the adobe.
Violet pours another
cup of coffee. As she
gazes at the floor,
she ponders the way
Jake made love to her
the night before. He
was rougher than usual,
and he scared her
though she kept it to herself.
She shudders thinking
about it, not because
of Jake's roughness
but because of the way
she liked the sensation
of lust heightened
with stark terror.
Just inches away,
beside a leg of the table,
she sees the shadow
of a thick-handed
scorpion. It doesn't
even faze her.

Prickly Pears

Violet's Mexican mother
steeped her in the ages
old secrets of the desert.

It is late August
and the tunas
of the prickly pears

have reddened
to deep magenta
the Aztecs used as dye.

With the bottom
of a halved plastic bottle,
Violet twists the tunas

off the pads, dodging
the angel fuzz stickers
clustered on the skins,

so fine the wind
can dislodge and blow
them by the hundreds

into her eyes. With tongs,
she turns the tunas
in a gas flame.

The stickers flare
and melt. She peels off
the skin with a paring knife.

Her nostrils flare
with the sweet, pungent
pulp of deep magenta.

The Color Violet

was palpable,
thick as pigment
from the palette
of an artist,
suffusing the dusk
of the day
she was born
like the dust
of a storm.
It came into the house
through the open
door and windows,
coloring the skin
of the midwife
and the *curandera*.
It even robed
the distant mountains,
the sky, the desert,
the very air,
caking everything
it touched, fracturing
into the letters
of her name.

3. He Likes the Space

Creosote

Every morning
at daybreak, Jake
takes a long walk
among the creosote.
He likes the space
between the plants,
allowing them
the water they need
for survival. Water

is scarce out here
as an issue-free
existence. Roots
of the creosote
are both shallow,
to slurp the moisture
of fifty square yards,
and deep, to reach
groundwater.

The tap roots
are tough enough
to penetrate caliche.
Jake loves the camphor-
like smell of creosote
after a monsoon rain,
ballooning his lungs
with the scent of plants
hundreds of years old.

Slumber

In the middle
of the night,
Violet wakes
with her open hand,
palm down, splayed
across Jake's chest.
She dares not

move her hand
as Jake might wake,
jerk up, and grope
for a ghost weapon.
His nightmares
usually begin
with a body tremor,

followed by muffled
gasps. She feels
the savage beating
of his heart
ticking in his body
like an IED
of solid muscle.

In His Dream

Jake is a black-
tailed jackrabbit.
His belly is flush
against the sand

in his scrape
beneath a scrub
of mesquite. The five
thousand stars

visible above him
are torches wielded
by a violent mob.
Hidden by but a wisp

of lacy leaves, he hears
the yelps of coyotes
drawing nearer with each
vicious tick of the clock.

He tries to move but can't,
helplessly vulnerable
to the timeless, red rite
of devourment.

Reveille

As Jake stirs awake,
the sun's red-orange fingers
are prying through

a window pane.
He winces in the glare.
Dislodging crumbs of sleep

from the corners
of his eyes, he hears
Violet's heavy breathing.

A platoon of blue quail
bursts into a reveille
of shrieks and two-noted

"Pecos" calls. Jake
reaches for his glasses
on the bedside table

and eases them to the bridge
of his nose, anxious about
which of his two distinct

pairs of eyes will gaze
upon the uncharted day
of gall and brutal light.

El Padre

(La Frontera*, far West Texas)

(* Spanish term: translated into English as "border")

1. The Pivotal Moment

Uncle Pedro

El Padre's admiration
of his mother's only brother
led him to become a priest.

Pedro was one of a handful
of Mexican priests
whose practice of exorcism

was sanctioned by Rome.
He took great pride
in his role as an exorcist,

ever mindful of the dangers
of such intimacy with Satan.
His gravelly baritone

matched the rough stones
rumbling in Satan's throat
measure for measure,

grinding them down
to impotent puffs
of powder.

The Hours

El Padre
contemplates the hours
of the Holy Sunday
during which he decided

to become a priest.
The pivotal moment
came at the end
of the Eucharist

when he smelled his breath
redolent with the flesh
and blood of Christ.
The sun shone

through the stained glass
as it had never
shone before,
pouring in cataracts

through the red and blue
robes of the Apostles,
bathing El Padre
in the silent miracle

of color. Not until
late the next day,
after his mouth
had cleansed itself

of every final trace
of the Host,
would El Padre
eat or drink.

Crucifixes

The massive one
in the sanctuary
was fashioned by an artisan

in Mexico who, the last decade
of his life, drove himself blind
carving, sanding, and painting it.

Their uprights and transverses
dominate the lives
of El Padre and his flock

as if anything oblique
is a cardinal sin.
In silver they slide

down the cleavage of virgins.
El Padre muses
the weight of the one

hanging from his neck.
Even the cane cholla*
heaped up against the steps

to the sanctuary is nothing
but a cluster of crude crucifixes
studded with thousands of thorns.

(*also know as "walking stick cactus")

Jacob's Staff

(also known as "Jacob cactus")

An hour before first light,
the day before Good Friday,
El Padre is at his desk
in his small rectory office,
working on his homily
for Easter Sunday.

The moonless night
leans against his window
like a huge black beast.
The feeble glow
of a Banker's Lamp
greens and shadows his face.

Stirred by the wind,
the thorns of the ocotillo
just outside the window
claw his concentration,
scraping panes like fingernails
dragged across a chalkboard.

El Padre pictures
its long stems perfect
for fencing, walking sticks;
its fat buds on the verge
of bursting into flowers
his parishioners will consume

and press over wounds
to slow bleeding;
flowers so palpable,
bathed in grace
crimson as the blood
of Christ.

2. In the Lake of Fire

Esperanza*

The daughter
of the gardener
of the church's grounds
sometimes wears yellow.
Every time she does so,
her yellow confounds El Padre,

dragging his mind
uncomfortably close
to the temptation
of butter, the sheen of gold,
and the molten pigment
of the brash, impudent sun.

It dissolves his resolve
in the lake of fire,
leaving him to question
his youthful surrender
to the unforgiving vow
of celibacy.

(*a flowering desert shrub)

The Confession

Her purity of heart
pierces the screen
between them
like rays of sunlight
bursting through stained glass.

The brightness
constricts the pupils
of El Padre's eyes
like nooses jerked taut,
leaving him almost blind.

Her kneeler creaks
with the sodden weight
of her remorse.
Through sobs and gasps,
her paltry sin emerges

like a faint smudge
on a silver crucifix
returned to spotlessness
with the gentle sweep
of a cloth. Beads of sweat

wobble in the creases
of El Padre's forehead,
and he shivers, crushed
beneath the tonnage of sins:
human, inconfessable.

Poinsettias

In El Padre's dream,
they grow, right before his eyes,
to great heights
all around the periphery
of the sanctuary,

crumbling its adobe bricks
and shattering
the stained-glass windows.
Inside the sanctuary,
they sprout from the oaken

pews and floor,
reaching the ceiling in minutes,
wrapping their branches
tight around the statues
of Christ and the Holy Virgin,

choking the sanctuary
with millions upon millions
of blood-red bracts,
bracts hallowed by the Aztecs
for miracles

of scarlet dye
and bringing down the fever
of bronze children
trembling in delirium,
gazing through a portal of death.

The Nightmare

sometimes comes, bleeding
into El Padre's psyche
like black ink into a blotter.

He is young, in the first
year of his priesthood.
The cathedral is old

and cavernous, like those
of Europe, jutting
from the grainy cityscapes

like dark, imposing shrines.
The cardinal has sent
him there, to study

the ways of his elders.
It is late one evening
and he has misplaced

his briefcase. Seeking it,
he hears in the distance
part of a conversation

between the monsignor
and a teen-aged choirboy.
Unseen and shaken,
he exits the church

into the night with nothing
to save him but a life

of hard, hard prayer
and the doubt-plagued
machinations of semantics.

3. Each Sacred Syllable

Pigeon's Blood*

In his dream,
he lifts the chalice

to his lips,
his soul readied

for the blood of Christ.
When he tilts it,

the blood hardens
and shatters

into a host
of gleaming stones.

(*the exceptional color of the Burmese Ruby)

The Homily

As El Padre
is preparing
the notes
for his homily,
the sun crests
a mountain
and a shaft

of sunlight crashes
through the glass
of the window,
leaving El Padre's
notes smoldering
in a hushed inferno.
The brightness

is palpable
and blinding.
El Padre turns
away from the glare,
closes his blanched
eyes, and feels
like a child

possessed
with the devil,
his flesh smarting
with lashes
from a bullwhip
of flung,
holy water.

At the Statue

Night has fallen
and the sanctuary
is aglow
with a hundred

burning candles.
Through the darkness,
El Padre sees
the two widows

kneeling at the statue
of the Holy Virgin.
Each is clad
head to toe in black

and a scarf
of black lace
is tied
beneath her chin.

The flickering candles
cast ominous shadows
on the ceiling.
El Padre shudders

at the urgency
of their whispered
Hail Marys,
and sees the rosaries

bleeding
through their fingers
like sparkling,
black rivers.

The High Latin Mass

Every night
before falling
asleep, El Padre
invokes fragments
of the rhythmic,

hypnotic chants
he's cherished
since childhood.
Diphthongs
loose themselves

from his throat
and flow
through his lips
like ghosts
of the departed.

He marvels
at the holiness
of each
sacred syllable,
unblemished

by its passage
through centuries,
swirling
in the chalice
of his soul.

Plácido

(La Frontera, far West Texas)

"No art, however minor, demands less than total dedication if you want to excel in it."

Leon Battista Alberti

I. His Birthing So Arduous

Plácido

From the moment
of conception
until his birth,

his mother was obsessed
with music.
She knew by rote

dozens of traditional
Mexican songs
sung to her

by her mother
and grandmother.
Blessed with a beautiful

voice, perfect pitch,
and the tremolo
of an opera diva,

she sang her way
to the contractions,
bedpost-gripping,

pushing, bleeding,
and screaming
of natural childbirth.

The Shroud

Plácido's mother,
by the time he reached
six months of age,
knew he was deaf.
She had stopped singing
after recovering

from his birthing,
his birthing so arduous
it almost took her
and Plácido's lives.
She also knew
he couldn't speak.

Silence shrouded him,
smothering birdsong,
wind-howl,
puppy-growl,
and the cooing
of his mother's voice.

Sensing the Heat

The energy
Plácido reserved
in not hearing
or speaking,

unbeknownst
to his mother
and grandmother,
began to feed

his sight and touch.
He saw the world
with the eyes
of raptors,

and his fingers
felt things
before the moment
of contact,

his fingers
sensitive
as the pits
on the heads

of diamondbacks
sensing the heat
of a candle flame
thirty feet away.

II. Caressing the Box

The Coloring Book

Its images were derived
from the drawings
of Orozco, Rivera, and Siqueiros.

Even at five years of age,
Plácido kept his colors
within the thin lines

on the roughly textured pages,
handling each pencil
as if it were a scalpel.

His grandmother, a retired
teacher, told his mother
he was a prodigy.

Before easing a pencil
by its sharpened tip
from the box, he would study

all of them for several minutes,
caressing the box
with both of his small hands

as if it were a tiny choir loft
pulsing with the rainbowed
voices of Benedictine nuns.

The Gift

His grandmother found it
in a used bookstore
and gave it to Plácido.

Though worn from use,
the book was filled
with vivid color plates

of the murals
of the Mexican masters.
From the time Plácido

first opened it,
he was mesmerized
by the shapes and colors,

the shapes and colors
so silken and alive
as he traced them

with his fingertips:
silken and alive
as the baby ravens

which trembled in his palms,
fallen from the short-lived
heaven of their nest.

In His Nightmare

the tattered book
of Mexican murals
is burning. As a wraith
turns a page, it erupts

into flame, melting
the brilliant colors,
the brilliant colors
running down the walls

in little rivers,
pooling on the marble
floors of monuments.
Plácido is desperate

to smother the flames
but can't move.
He just freezes on his bed
with his mouth

locked wide-open,
shattering the darkness
with the palpable
silence of his screaming.

III. But Inches from His Fingers

The Thick-handed Scorpion

To draw it,
Plácido kept it
in a yellow flower pot
whose shiny interior

was too slick
for the scorpion
to crawl out.
He kept it only

until his drawing
was finished,
and then returned it
to its desert habitat.

When he showed his art
to his mother, she gasped,
recoiling from the drawing,
as if her son,

with his meticulous
craftsmanship,
had duplicated the very
liveliness of his model,

bestowing it with breath
and every gossamery hair
jutting from the deadliness
of its stinger.

On Paper and Woven Cotton

By the age of three,
Plácido had taught himself
to lip-read, sign, and to read.
Homeschooled

by his grandmother,
he devoured the books
within his reach, especially
literature and art books.

By the age of six,
he relished books
about art history
and the properties of color.

When not reading he drew
and painted, progressing
from colored pencils
to watercolor and acrylic,

competent with all three
by the age of thirteen.
The lenses of his glasses,
from one year to the next,

began to gradually thicken,
so concentrated was his focus
in the application of color
on paper and woven cotton.

On His Sixteenth Birthday

His mother trembled
handing him the thick,
unopened letter,

the letter of his acceptance
into the art institute
in Mexico City, on a full

scholarship. They wept
tears of joy, his mother's
bittersweet with the news

of his imminent departure;
his, not as much for study
with the masters

as the proximity
of the school to the palaces
and monuments housing

the grand murals quaking,
breathing, and smelling
but inches from his fingers.

Drawing Class

As Plácido drew,
his pencil was guided
by the hand of Orozco.

All of Mexican history
dwelt in the lead
of the pencil, smeared

from the wooden body
like desiccated blood.
Plácido drew

oblivious
of the suggestions
of his master instructor,

trusting instead
the pulsing exactitude
of Orozco.

Pecos

(Terlingua, far West Texas)

in memory of Beefy, my loyal Shetland Sheepdog,
&
for Pecos, my loyal Long-haired Chihuahua

"All knowledge, the totality of all questions and all answers, is contained in the *dog*."

Franz Kafka

Introduction

Larry D. Thomas, a former Texas Poet Laureate, is a true friend of *Right Hand Pointing*. Larry doesn't publish much in online journals, and yet his poems have appeared in many issues of *RHP* and this is his 11th online chapbook with us. It's an honor that Larry entrusts his work to us. As a point of personal privilege, I will say that a wonderful part of my life as an editor has been to develop relationships with several people who are my favorite poets. Larry is one of those.

Larry's work is not typical of what appears at *RHP*. I'm not smart enough to be able to articulate how it's atypical, but it is. The poems are thoroughly Texan, and thoroughly American. They are accessible, but with no hint of the compromise that accessibility sometimes requires. What I think I love most about Larry's work is the exquisite sensitivity to the lives of people. People we might think of as common and ordinary, but who are anything but. We've published Larry's work about miners, war veterans, and all sorts of people who live outside the mainstream of society.

The poems in *Pecos* are human-and-dog poems, presented here in spite of our ban on pet poems. Have you had enough human-and-dog poems? Right. Me neither.

I'm reminded of Mark Doty's wonderful book, *Dog Years: A Memoir,* about two dogs who were with him and his partner as the partner died of AIDS. And then, of course, the dogs died, and there was more grief for Doty.

Dogs die, and that presents a problem. (People die too, but I'd rather not talk about that right now.) In 2007, I attended a reading Doty did from *Dog Years* at the Harvard Bookstore. During the Q&A, a man admitted he was puzzled that dog owners develop these deep bonds with their dogs and then go through terrible grief when their dogs die and then they turn around and get more dogs and on the cycle goes.

Everyone in the room chuckled except Mark Doty who, without hesitation, said "You know, the agreement to participate in this life is a pact with grief."

Here's what I took home from that. The agreement to participate in this life is a pact with grief.

I know you'll enjoy this little collection of 10 poems from our friend Larry D. Thomas.

Dale Wisely

Flush

Cleatus sits on the shack porch,
arching the sand with the dangling heel
of his boot. Pecos, his retired cow dog,
lies flush against Cleatus' outer thigh,
fighting the proverbial demon of sleep.
Cleatus' hand, buried in Pecos' fur,
rises and falls with Pecos' breathing.
As he feels for Pecos' heartbeat,
he feels instead his own, throbbing
in a cage of ribs they've shared
since Pecos was a puppy.

Pecos

First light startles him
as if it were the scent
of a jackrabbit.
He stretches his blue merle,
arthritic legs,
rolls over on his stomach,
and rises to his paws
slowly as the red-orange sun'll
heave itself over the horizon.
He eases to the side
of Cleatus' half-bed,
sniffs Cleatus' breath,
and jumpstarts him awake
with the slobbery, swirling
battery of his tongue.

Fur

Each morning,
when Cleatus gazes
into his bathroom mirror,
he notices the increasing
bushiness of his eyebrows
and the lengthening hairs
on the tops of his ears
and on his earlobes.
As he and Pecos
begin their morning walk
side by side, each moves
with a slight gimp
indistinguishable from that
of the other, a slight gimp
stemming from a touch
of arthritis. The fur of each
gleams with morning sun
like the filaments in light bulbs
heated to incandescence,
these two aged creatures
on their walk in the desert,
set apart but by the number
of their furred, rickety legs.

Grub

For their jerky,
Cleatus slices beef into strips
for drying in the sun.
He boils pinto beans
in an old black pot
once the favorite of his mother,
an old black pot
lumpy as homemade soap.
Cleatus cherishes his mother's
cast-iron skillet, especially
the way he never has to wash it;
the way, with nothing
but heat in the oven,
it works its magic,
turning meal, eggs, buttermilk,
lard, baking soda,
and a pinch of salt
into the steaming,
brittle miracle of cornbread.

Thorns

The big thorns
hardened on a branch
of dead mesquite
are only seemingly the nastiest.
Cleatus' heart muscle still smarts
from the thick, long, memory-thorns
of his dead wife's stillness:
of Smoke, the best cow horse
he ever had till he angrily
ran him down the slope
of an arroyo too rocky and steep,
fracturing Smoke's leg
beyond any hope of healing:
the thick, long, memory-thorns
dwarfing the deep ones
which took pliers
to pull from the pads of Pecos.

Ice Fog

On cold mornings,
Cleatus reminisces about
the three-day ice fog.
He still hears mesquite
and ocotillo branches
cracking from trunks
and distant power poles
snapping like matchsticks.
He had but Smoke and Pecos
to help him herd cattle to shelter
and still sees Pecos running
in and out of view, tightening
an illusory rope around the herd:
Pecos running in and out of view,
whooshing like a tireless
blue phantom.

Death

is the orange-red sun
sliding into the darkness
like legs into long johns
on cold winter nights.
Doctors and drugs, to Far
West Texans, are anathemas.
Like old cow dogs who wander
deep into the pasture to die
beneath a swirl of merciful vultures,
old cowhands who take sick
just take sick, rest as much
as possible, and swill
a little whiskey for pain.
Cleatus' dad's old dog, Blue,
who eked out a hard life
of eighteen years, lay dead
in the pasture for weeks
before two cowhands found him.
It was as if old Blue
planned it that way
to ease the grief of Cleatus' dad,
old Blue mostly desert
by the time they spotted him,
barely enough bones for a grave.

Rose

On the floor, on a folded
saddle blanket beside the head
of Cleatus' bed, Pecos snores.
Jerking awake, Cleatus squints
and then opens and closes
his eyes several times, to focus.
He thinks he sees
in the moonglow,
beneath Pecos' nose,
a faint, misshapen rose.
a rose but a blush of pink,
a rose so faint it's
scarcely there at all.

Cleatus Muses

the moon which tonight
makes Pecos cast a shadow
so dark Cleatus thinks he sees it spasm.
When full, its light stuns the shack
like the laying on of frosty hands,
blessing man and dog or waking them
to a netherworld where they reel,
caring less whether it's the bright
light of death or simply another day
graced with the staticky transmission
of "Waiting 'Round to Die."*

(*song by Townes Van Zandt)

First Light Creeps

into the shack, surreptitious
as the onset of dementia.
Each gratuitous morning,
in marvelous minutes,
lengthens the time
Cleatus and Pecos find themselves
strangely suspended in a state
half-sleep and half-wakefulness.
The cataracts, clouding
and suffusing their lenses with light,
enhance the strangeness
of the purgatorial state:
the state of sleep-waking:
the strangeness of floating
through the fleece-like
clouds of rapture.

"The Emperor of Ice-Cream"

(after the poem by Wallace Stevens)

"The only emperor is the emperor of ice-cream."

Wallace Stevens

1.

He smiles,
musing the white,
concupiscent curls
of his wig.

2.

His family tree
is the epitome
of parsimony:
King Cream,
Queen Sugar,
Grand Duke Vanilla,
and Grand Duchess Milk.

3.

Iciness
is the favorite
of his narcissistic
virtues.

4.

Some Caribbeans
celebrate death
with his gratuitous
freezing of the brain.

5.

He regards
the heart's warmth
the deadliest
of cardinal sins.

6.

His private daydreams
are tormented with thoughts
of vapor, freezer burn,
and the enticing battalions
of the neighboring
Kingdoms of Strawberry
and Dark Chocolate.

7.

He gasps
with recurring nightmares
disturbing as petulant,
stubborn subjects.

8.

But the thought of him
deluges the seared,
treasonous mouth.

9.

The tongue,
in any
of its myriad
applications,
tops the burgeoning
list of his fears.

10.

His subjects
cherish the concave
dangers of their spoons.

Luz

(a demanding, elusive, and indomitable muse)

1.

Her voice
is the blue-black sheen
of ravens.

2.

For over a century,
in an abandoned
quicksilver mine shaft
on the outskirts
of unincorporated Terlingua
in Far West Texas,
she has lived
and plied the awe and wonder
of her trade.

3.

Her legless bed frame
of antique mesquite
rests firmly
on the mine shaft floor.
She sleeps
on the onionskin pages
torn from the spines
of a thousand
discarded Bibles.
The red-lettered
words of Jesus
complement the red cinnabar
of the mine shaft walls
where quicksilver looms
like melted stars.

4.

When a toddler,
which she never
literally was,
she was obsessed
with wooden alphabet blocks,
especially the red,
yellow, blue and green
colors of the letters.
First, she picked up the red "A."
After fondling it
with her chubby fingers
for fifty million years,
she laid it gently down
and picked up the green "B."

5.

Checkers
is her favorite game.
She plays
only herself.
Her checkerboard
was a gift
from an elderly curandero
she stumbled upon
while hiking
the Sierra Madre Oriental.
He fashioned the squares
from black onyx
and hard white limestone.
Her checkers pieces
are light and shadow.

6.

She prides herself
in reciting backwards
and from memory,
to her walls of cinnabar,
every word
of Shakespeare's tragedies.

7.

When a young woman,
although she abhors
the word "young"
in whatever context
an idiot places it,
her only companions
were Greek
and Roman goddesses.
She was always leery
of the gods.

8.

She reads
at the speed
of light.
The only thing
she has ever forgotten
is forgetfulness.

9.

Even the conjuring
of the word "cannot"
detonates her
into a terrifying rage.
When raging,
she plagues her subject
with nightmares,
delirium,
and profuse sweating.

10.

She is never pleased
with her subject's
greatest achievements,
demanding perfection
from his erring,
human self.

11.

Silent as neon gas
illuming a glass tube,
she dyes the psyche
of her subject
indelibly with rapture
and amaranthine want.

About the Author

Larry D. Thomas, a member of the Texas Institute of Letters and the 2008 Texas Poet Laureate, has published thirty-five collections of poetry, twenty of which are print books and fifteen of which are electronic. His most recent print publication is *The Innkeeper*, released by Mouthfeel Press in early 2018.

Thomas has received a number of prizes and awards for his poetry, including the nomination of his poetry collection, *Stark Beauty*, for the 2007 Poets' Prize (Nicholas Roerich Museum). His *Larry D. Thomas: New and Selected Poems*, published by Texas Christian University Press in 2008 as part of the TCU Texas Poets Laureate Series, was longlisted for the 2008 National Book Award (the 2013 longlistees were the first to be announced to the general public). Additionally, his poetry books have been awarded two *Texas Review* Poetry Prizes (2001 and 2004), two Western Heritage Wrangler Awards (2003 and 2015), the 2004 Violet Crown Award (Writers' League of Texas), and two Violet Crown Award Finalist citations.

www.ingramcontent.com/pod-product-compliance
Lightning Source LLC
Chambersburg PA
CBHW021147160426
43194CB00007B/716